Maybe Swearing Will Help

This Coloring Book belongs to:

....

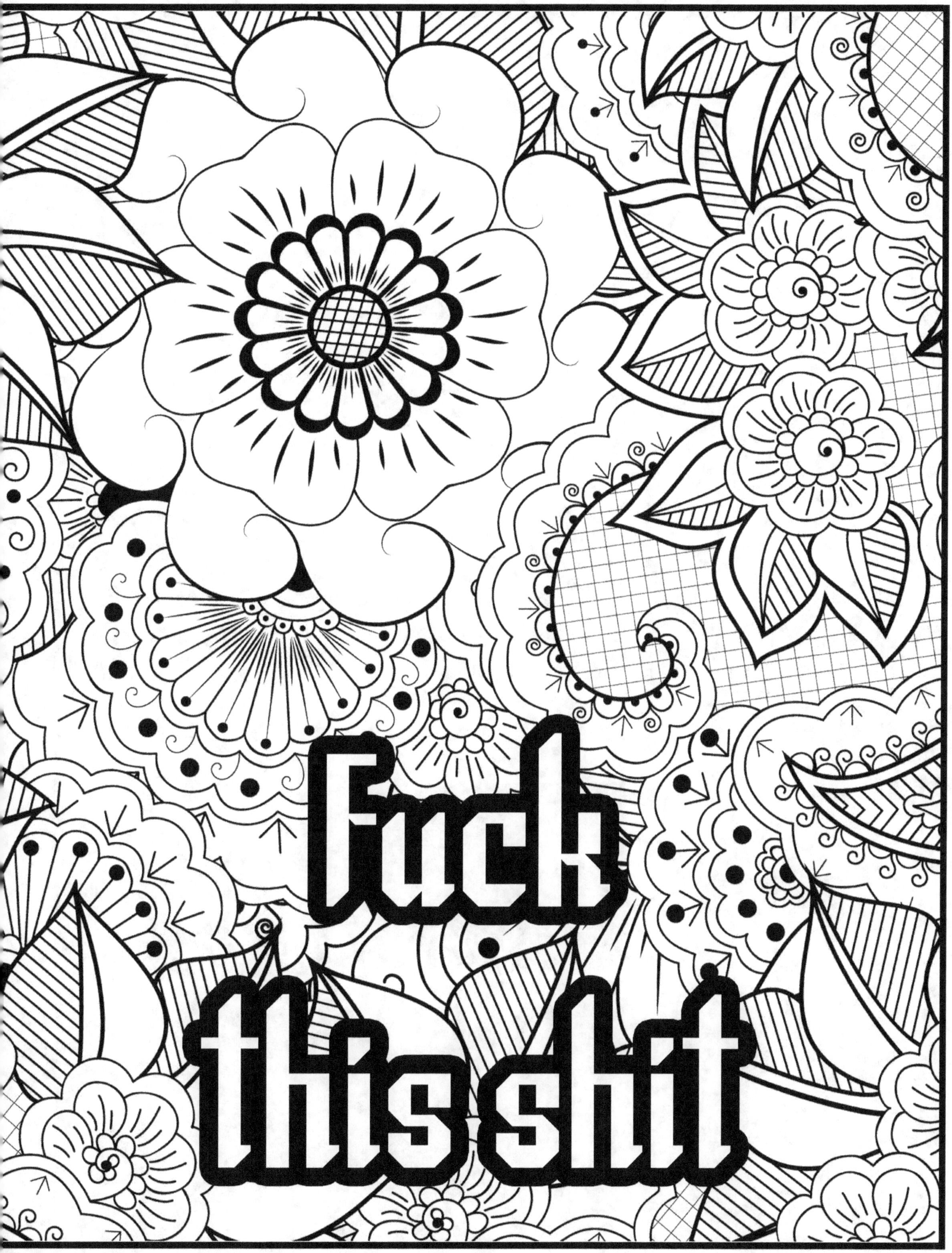
Fuck
this shit

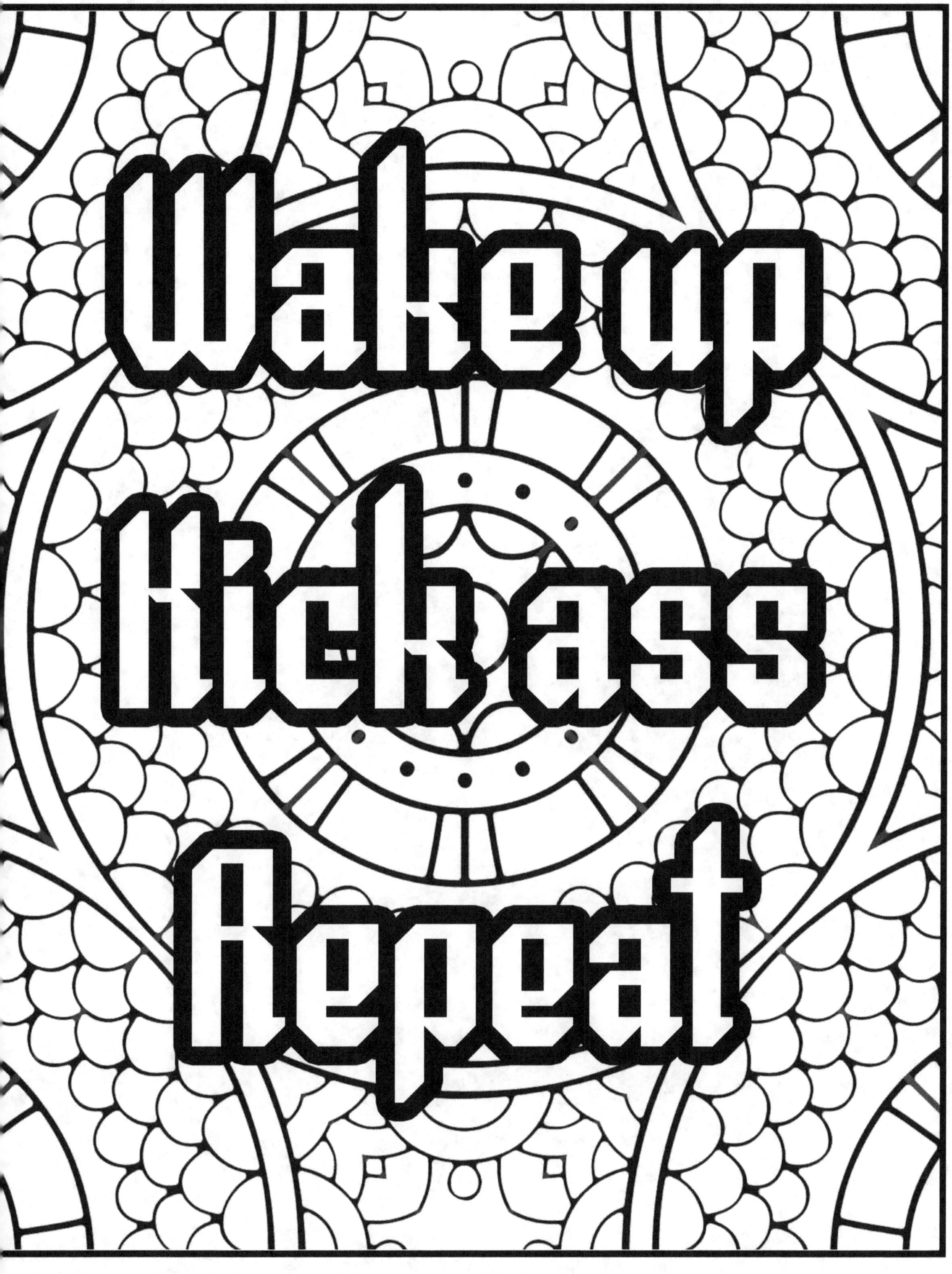
Wake up
Kick ass
Repeat

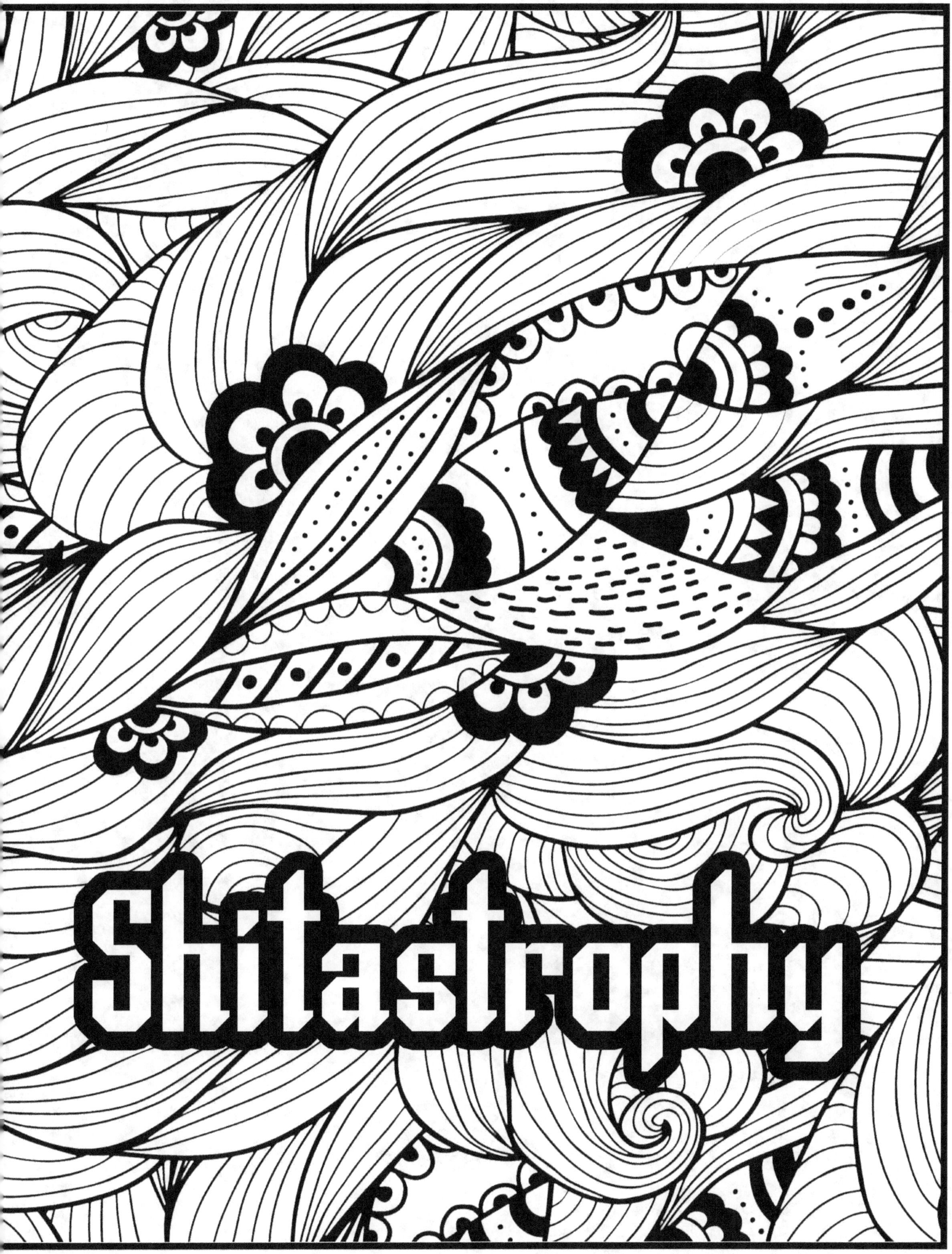
Shitastrophy

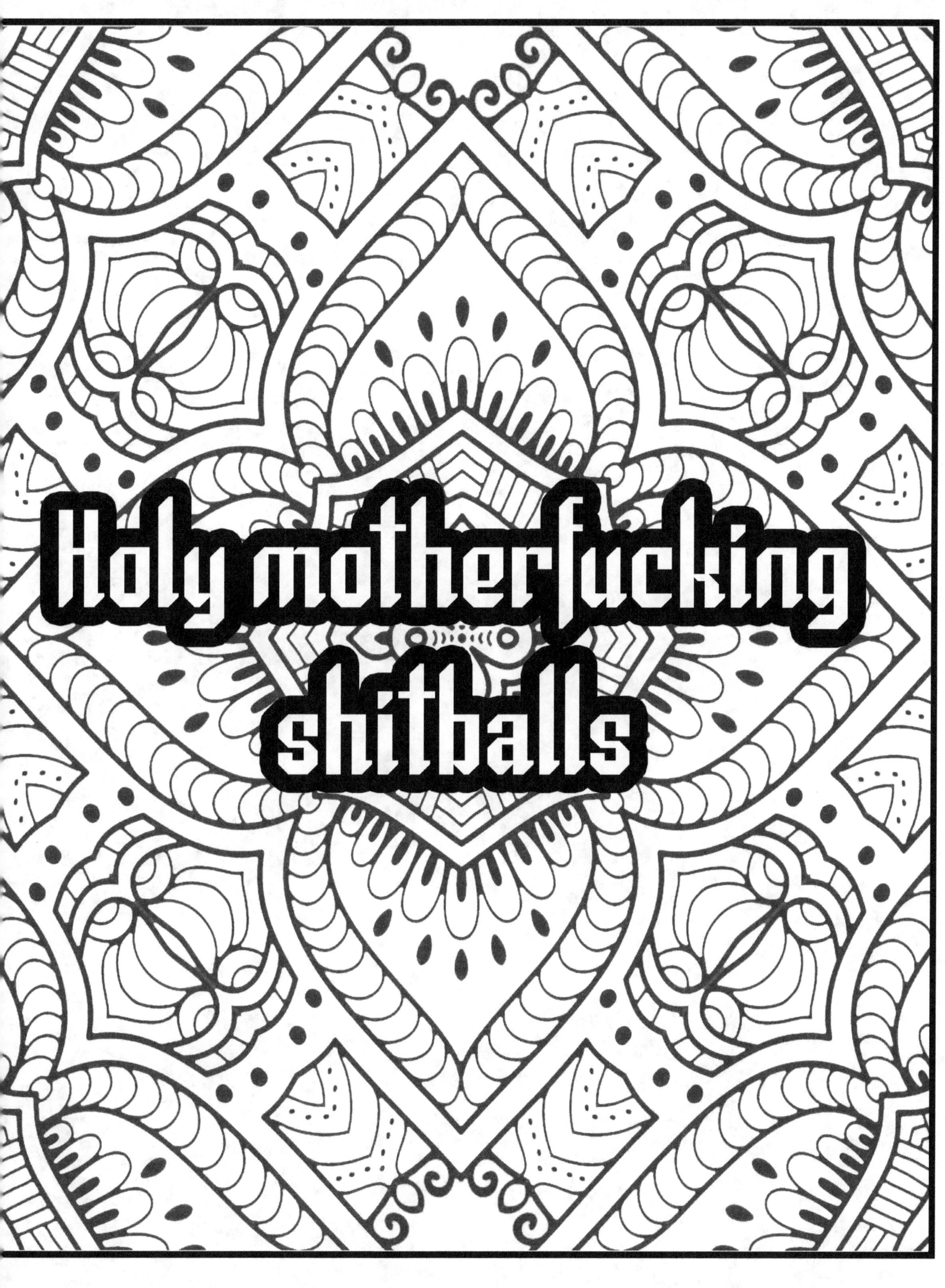
Holy motherfucking
shitballs

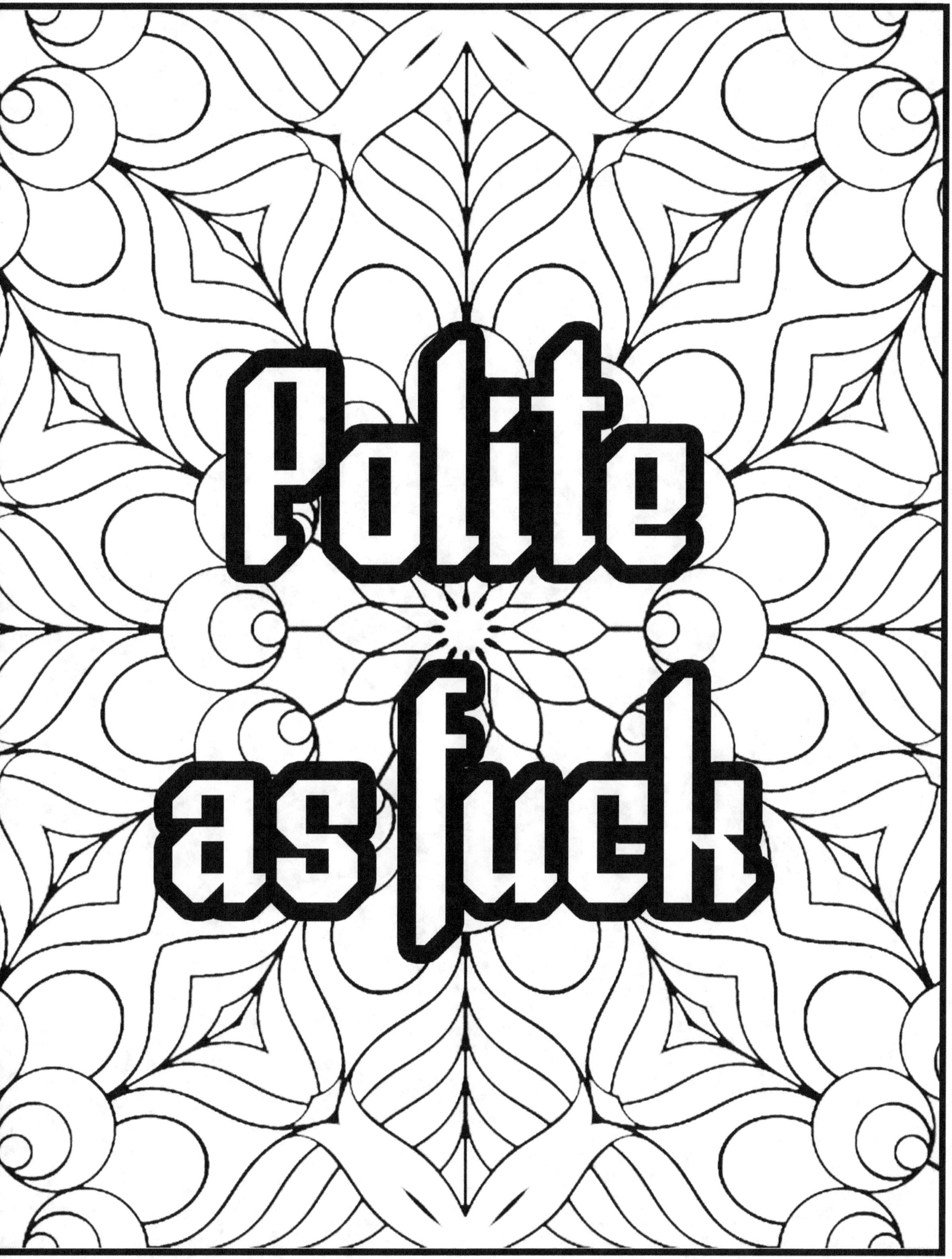
Polite
as fuck

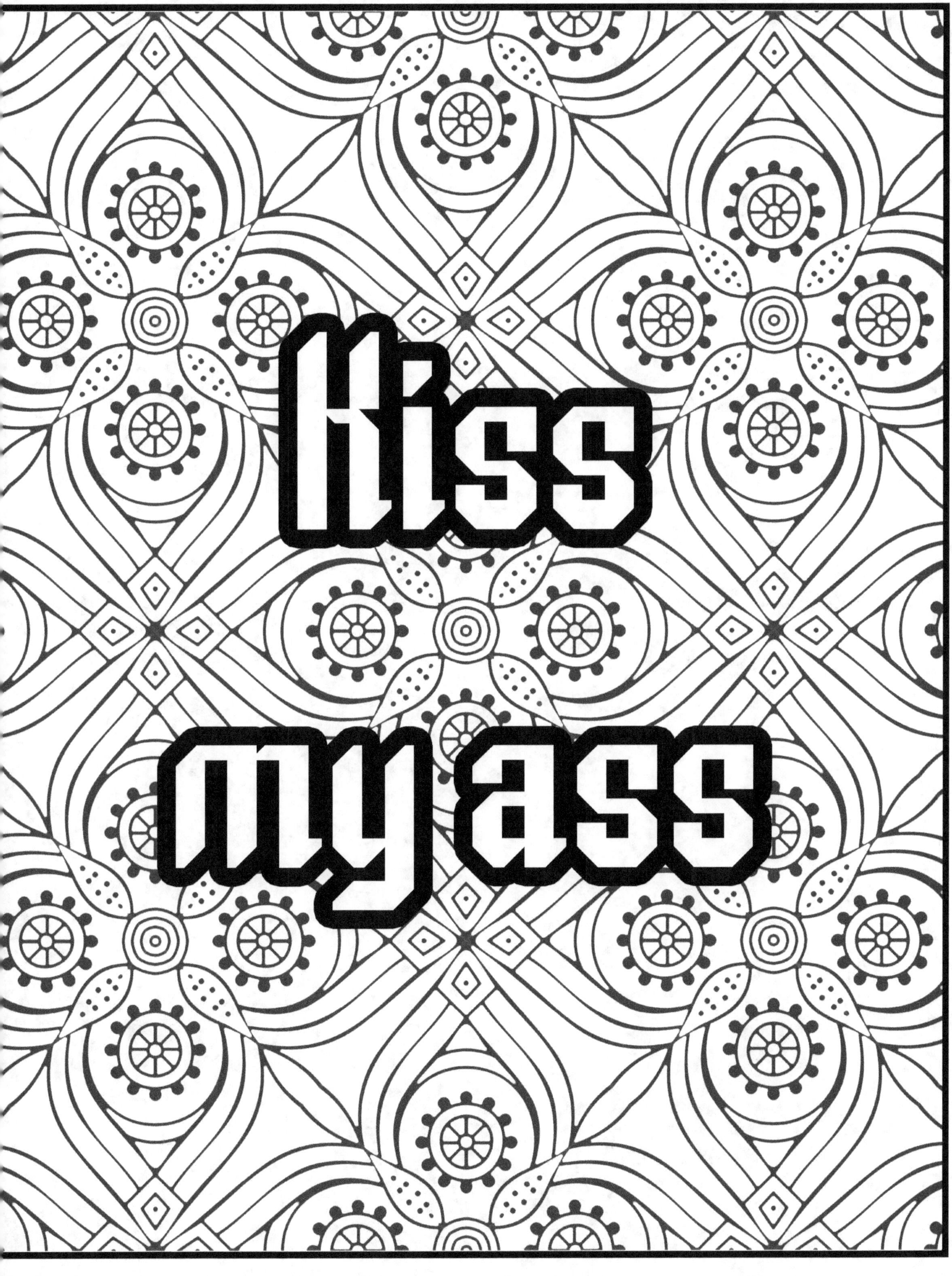
kiss
my ass

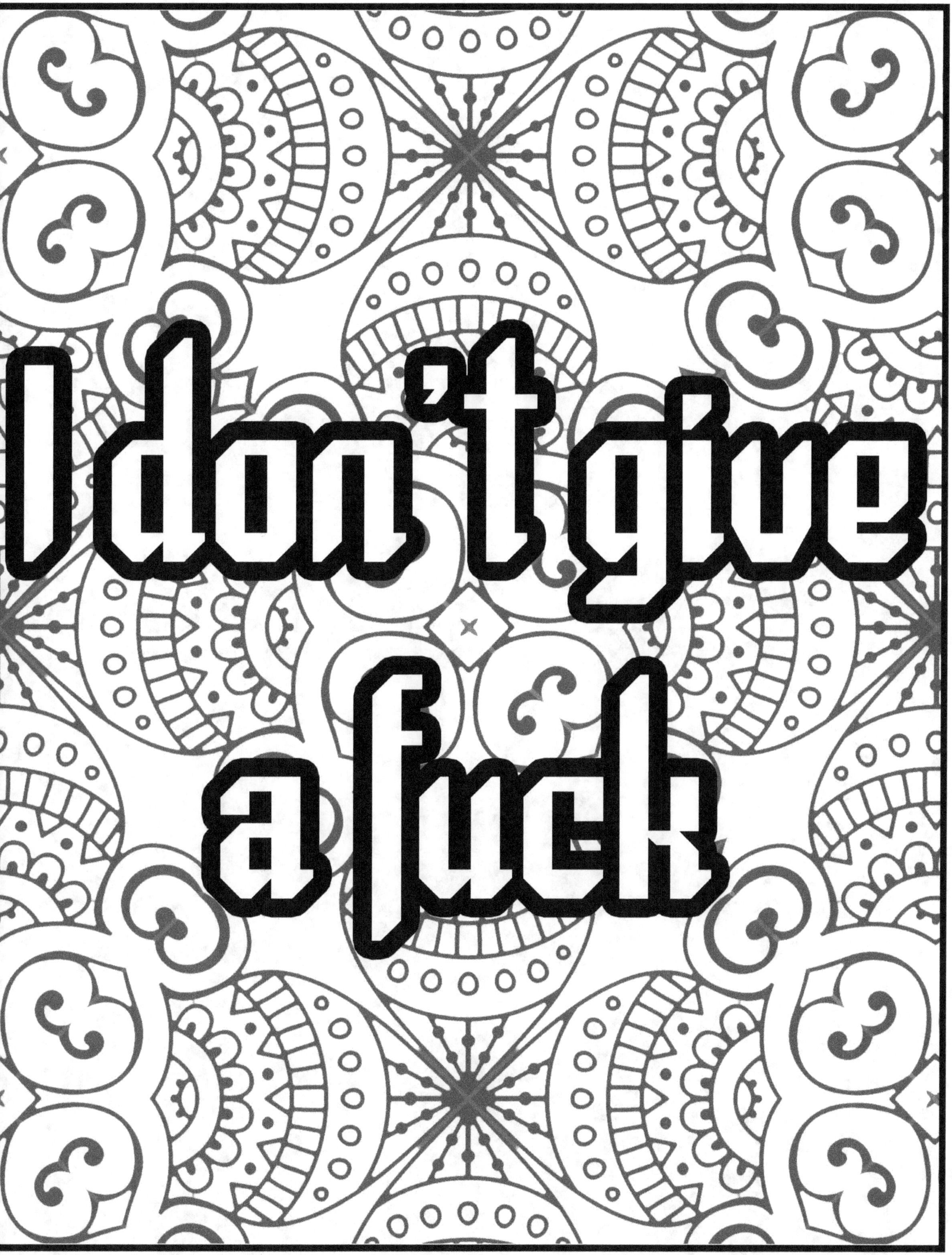
I don't give
a fuck

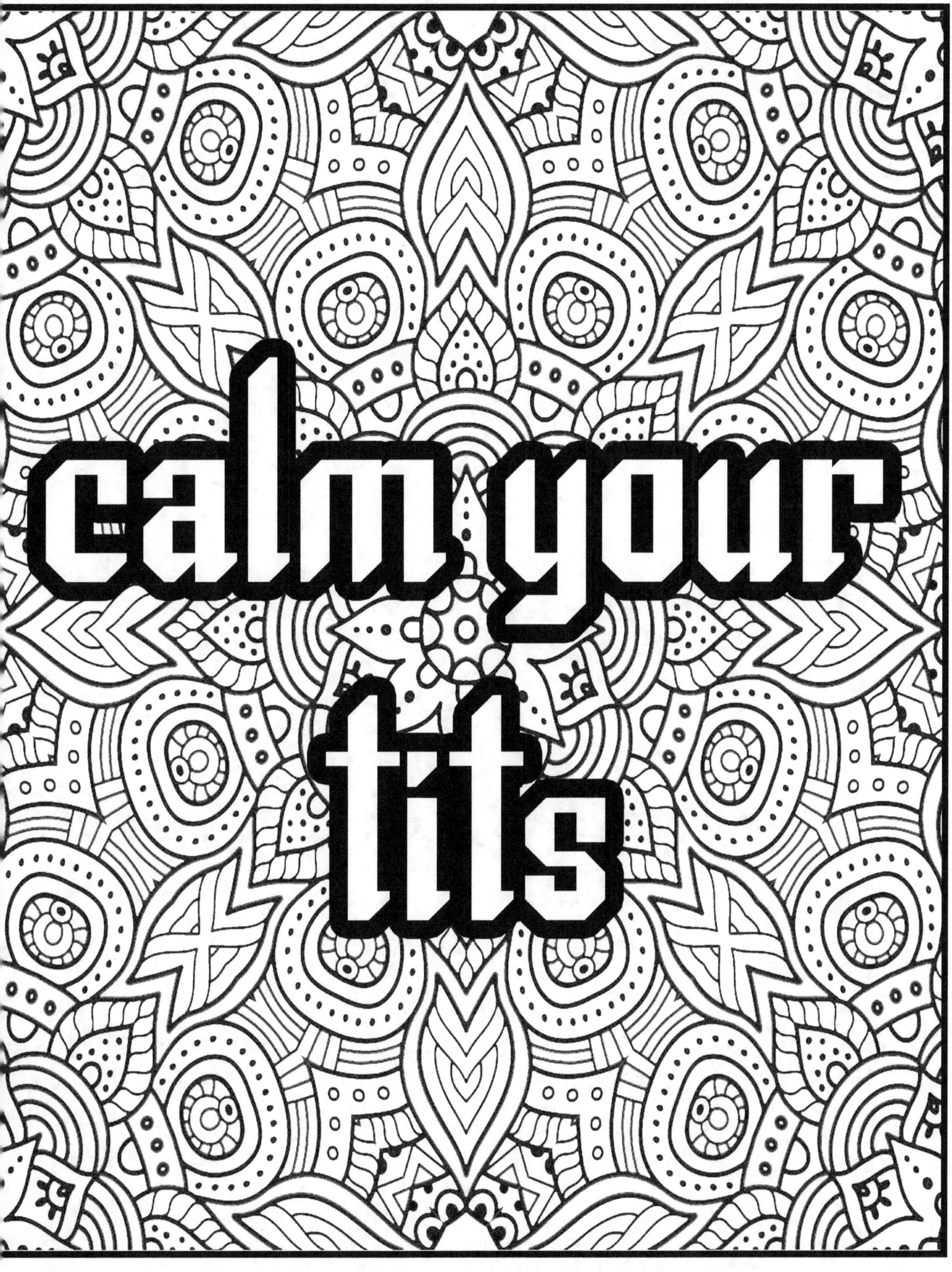
calm your
tits

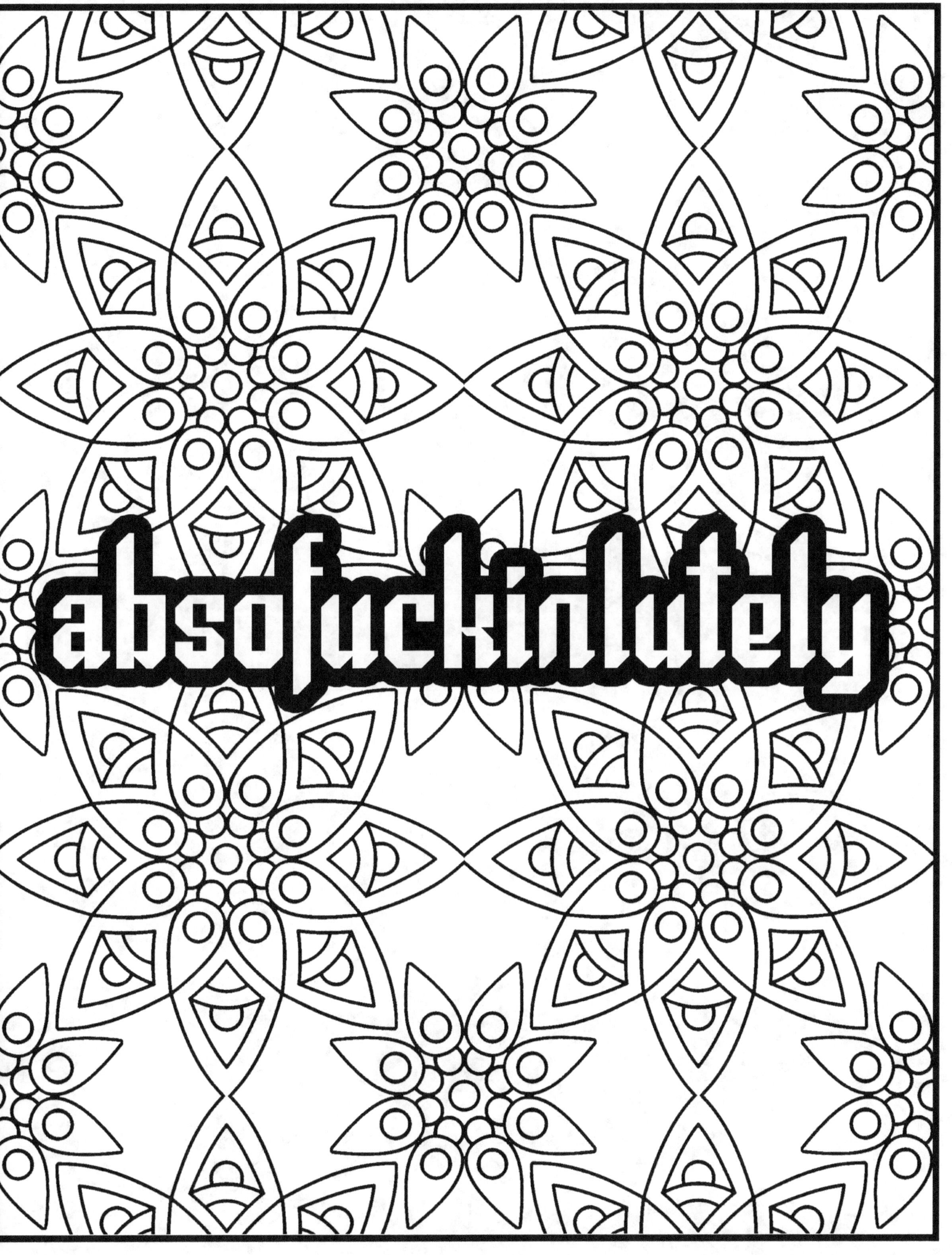
absofuckinlutely

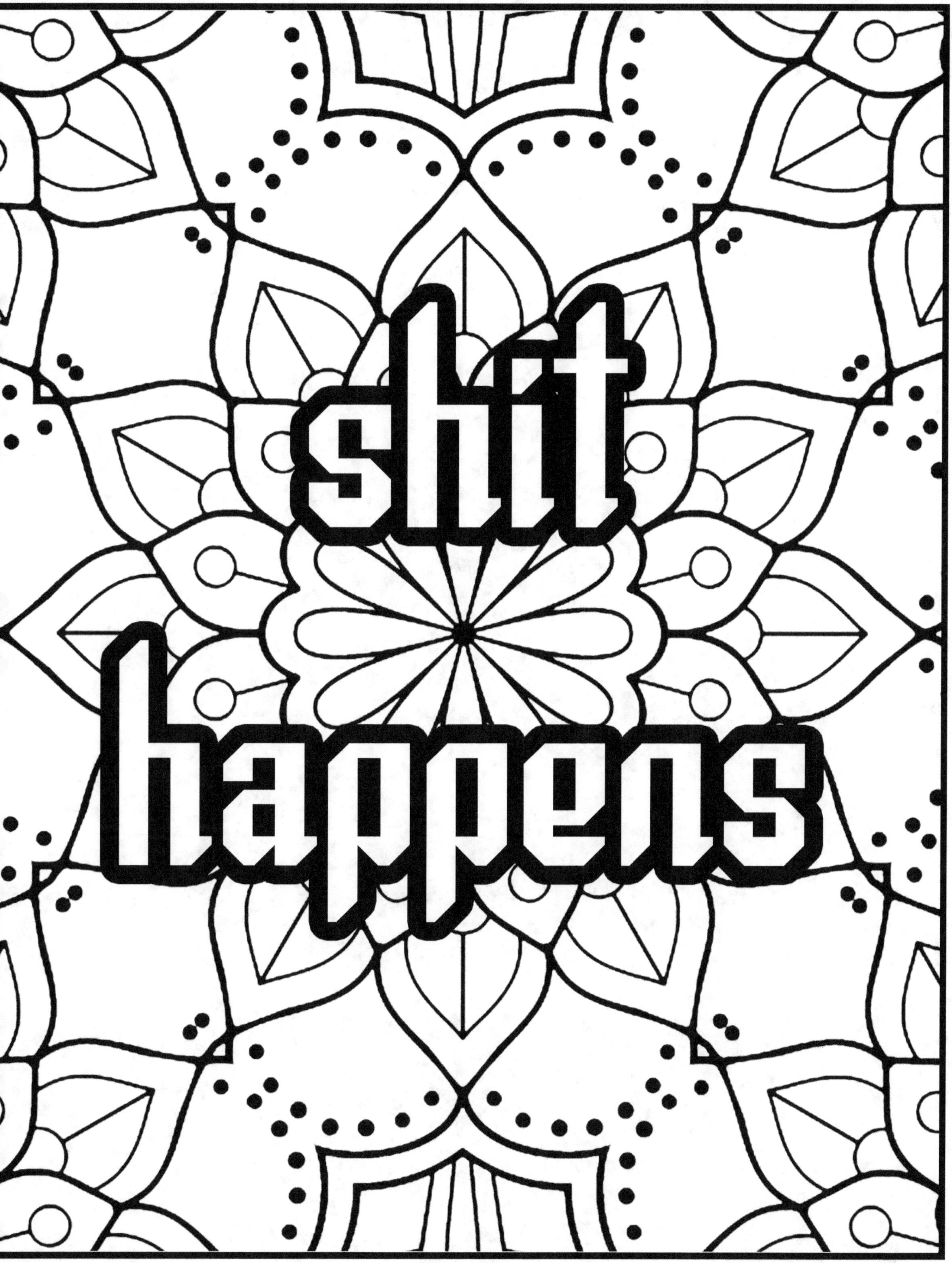
shit
happens

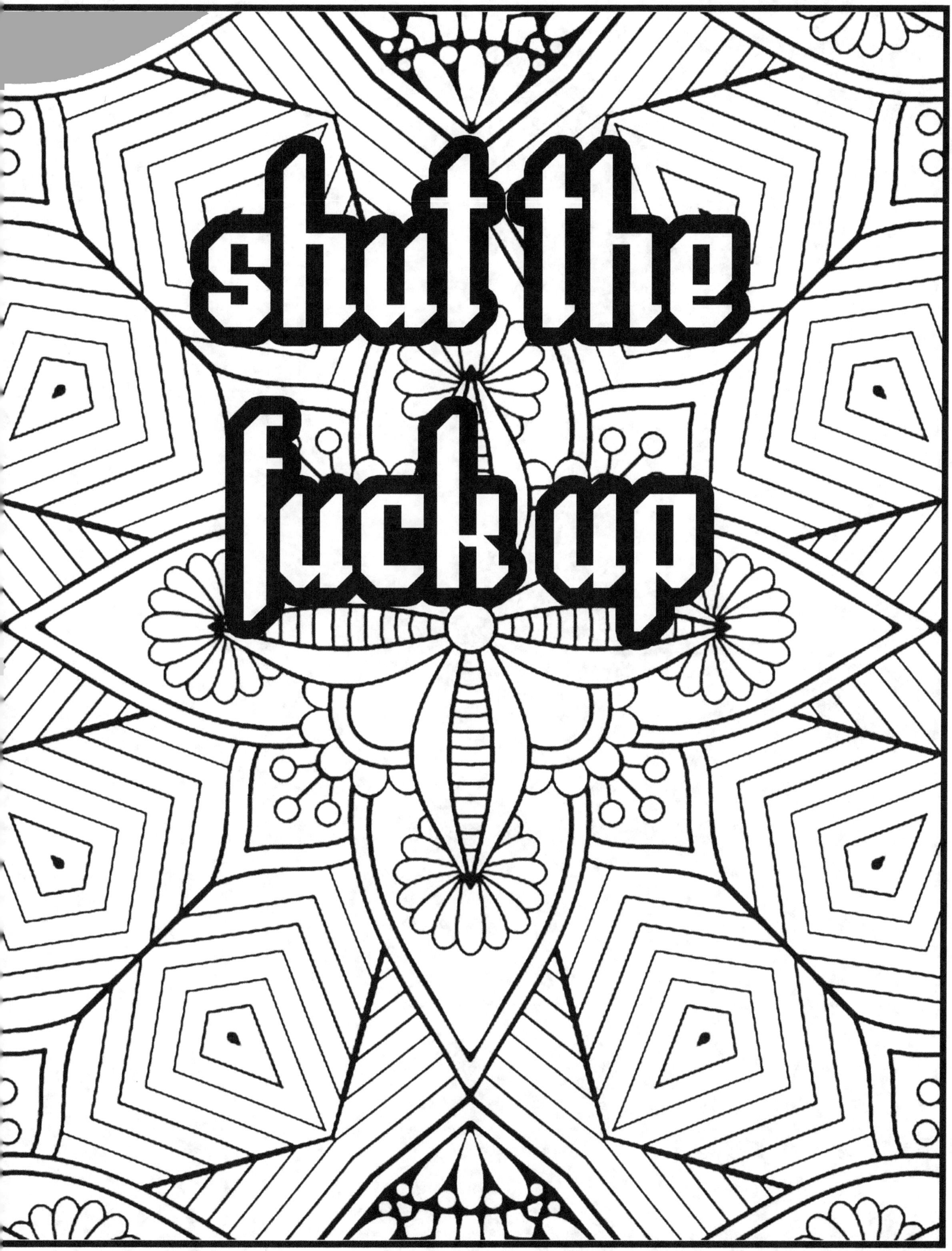
shut the
fuck up

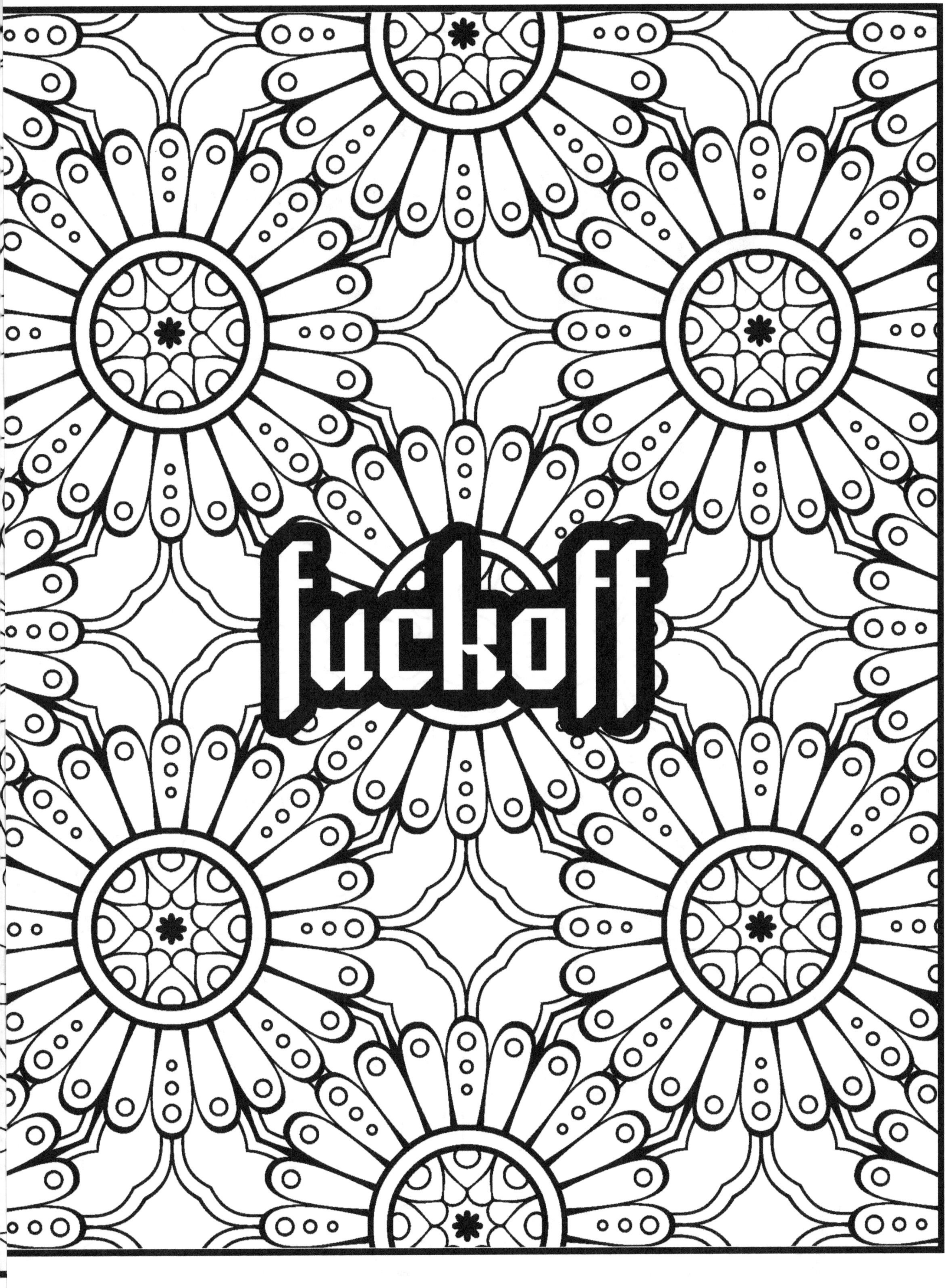
fuckoff

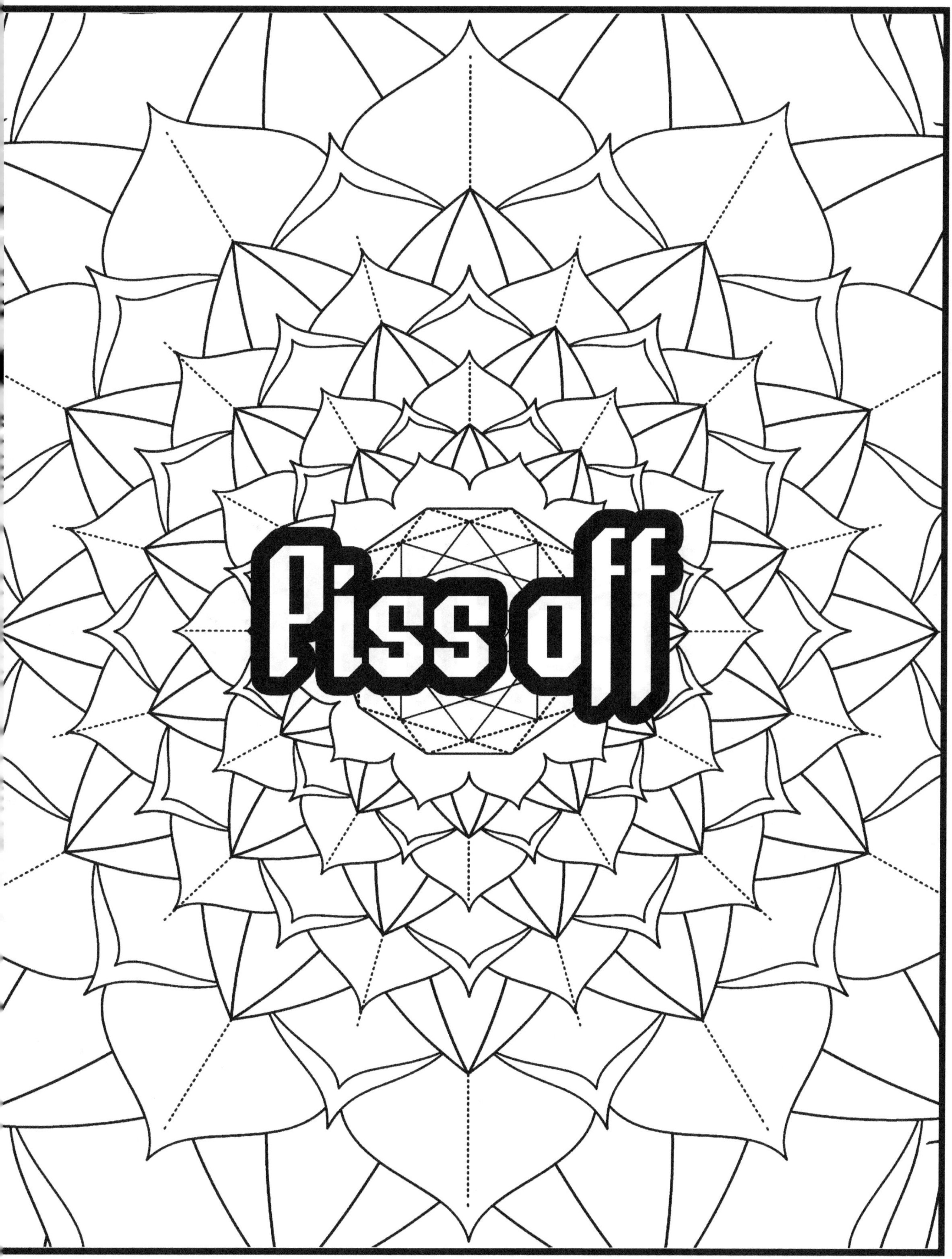
Piss off

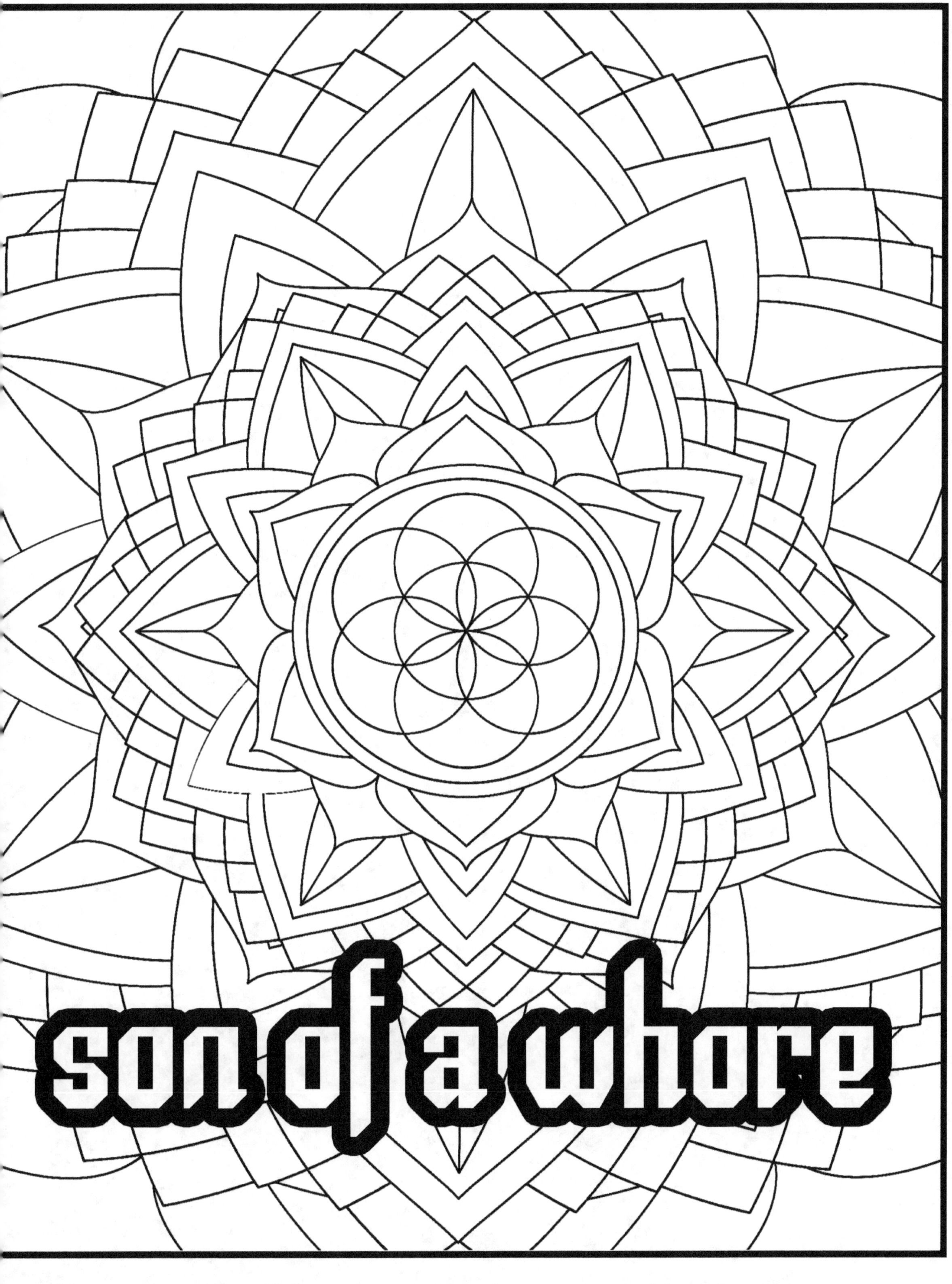
son of a whore

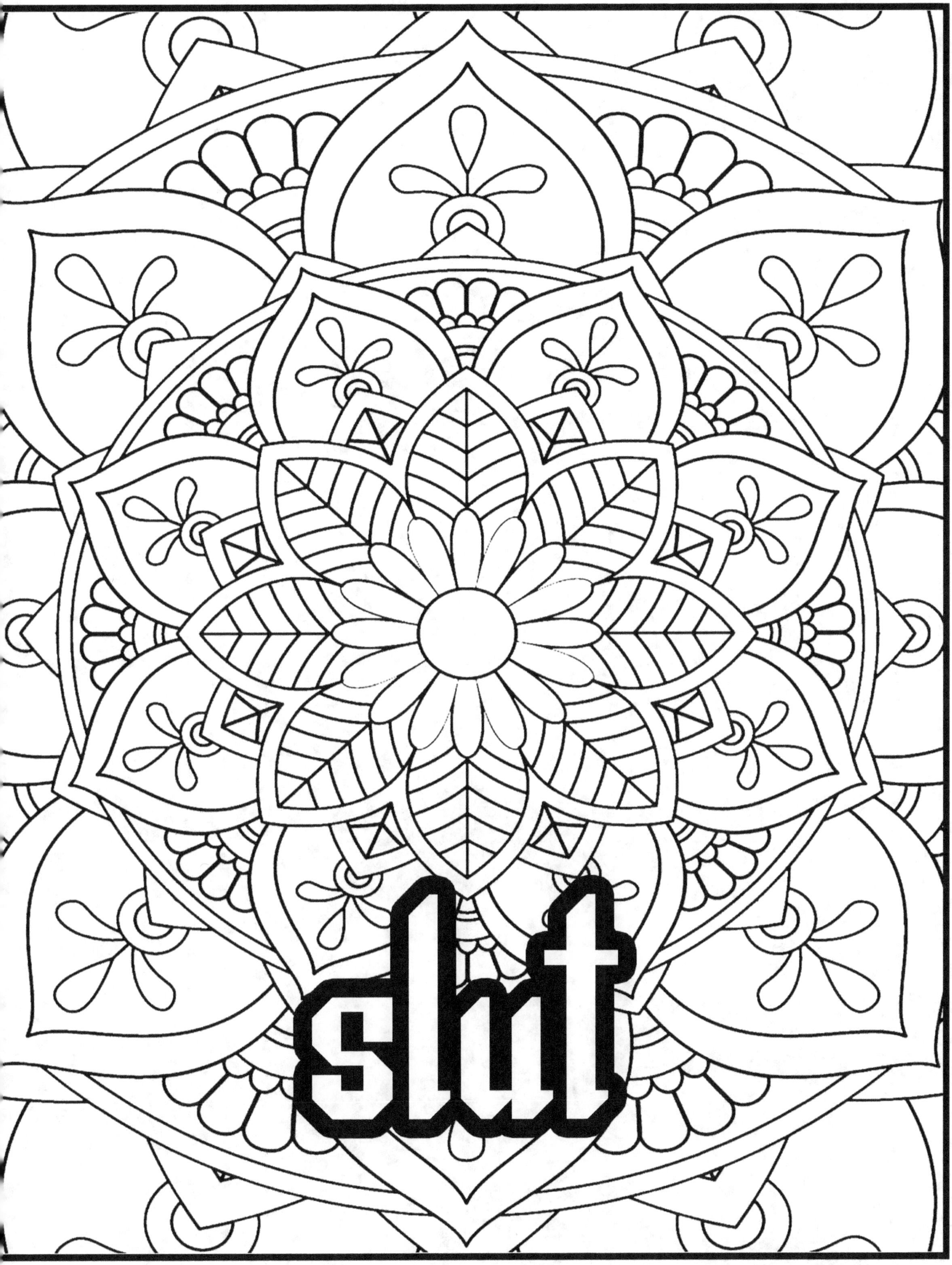
slut

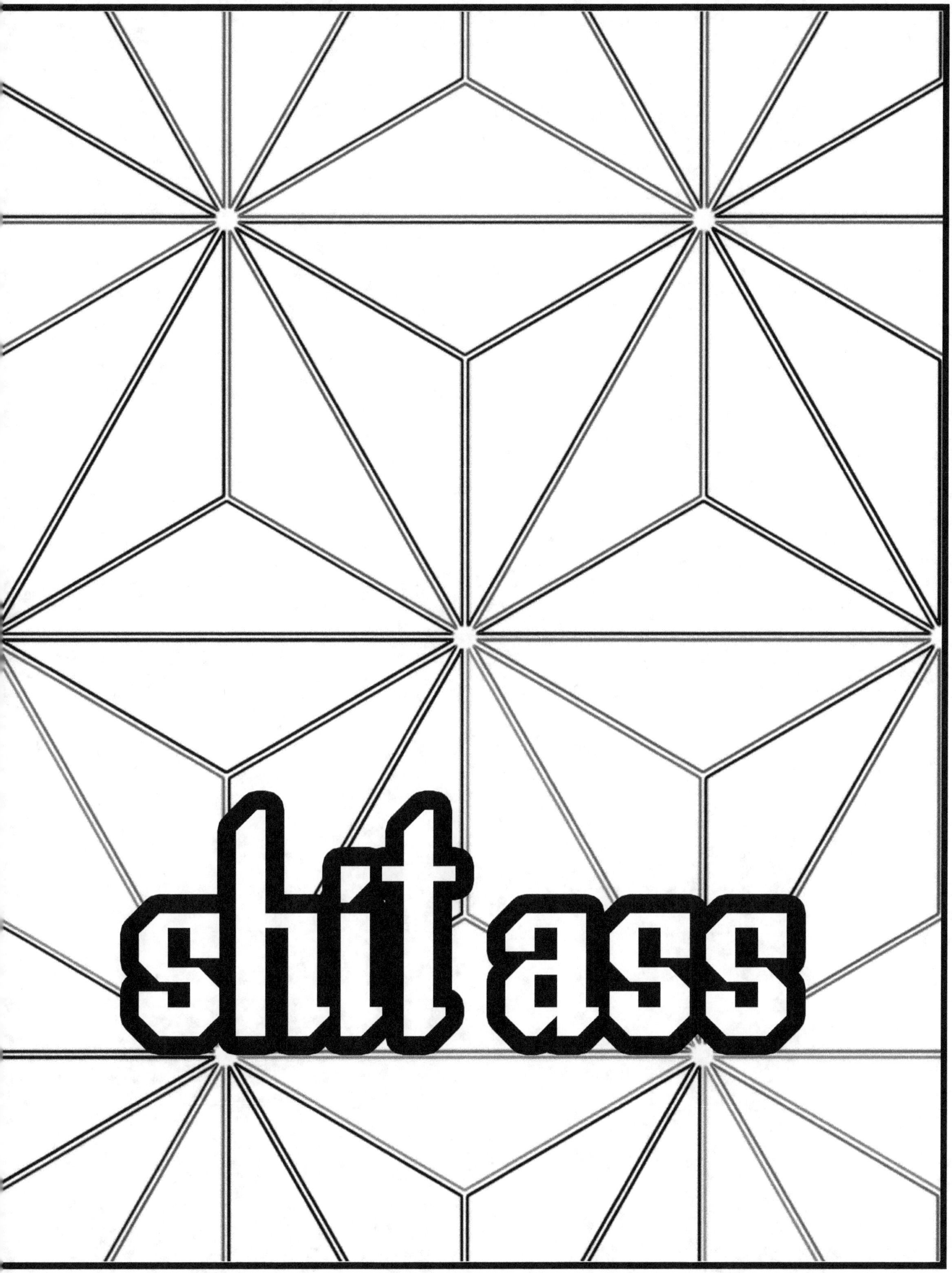
shit ass

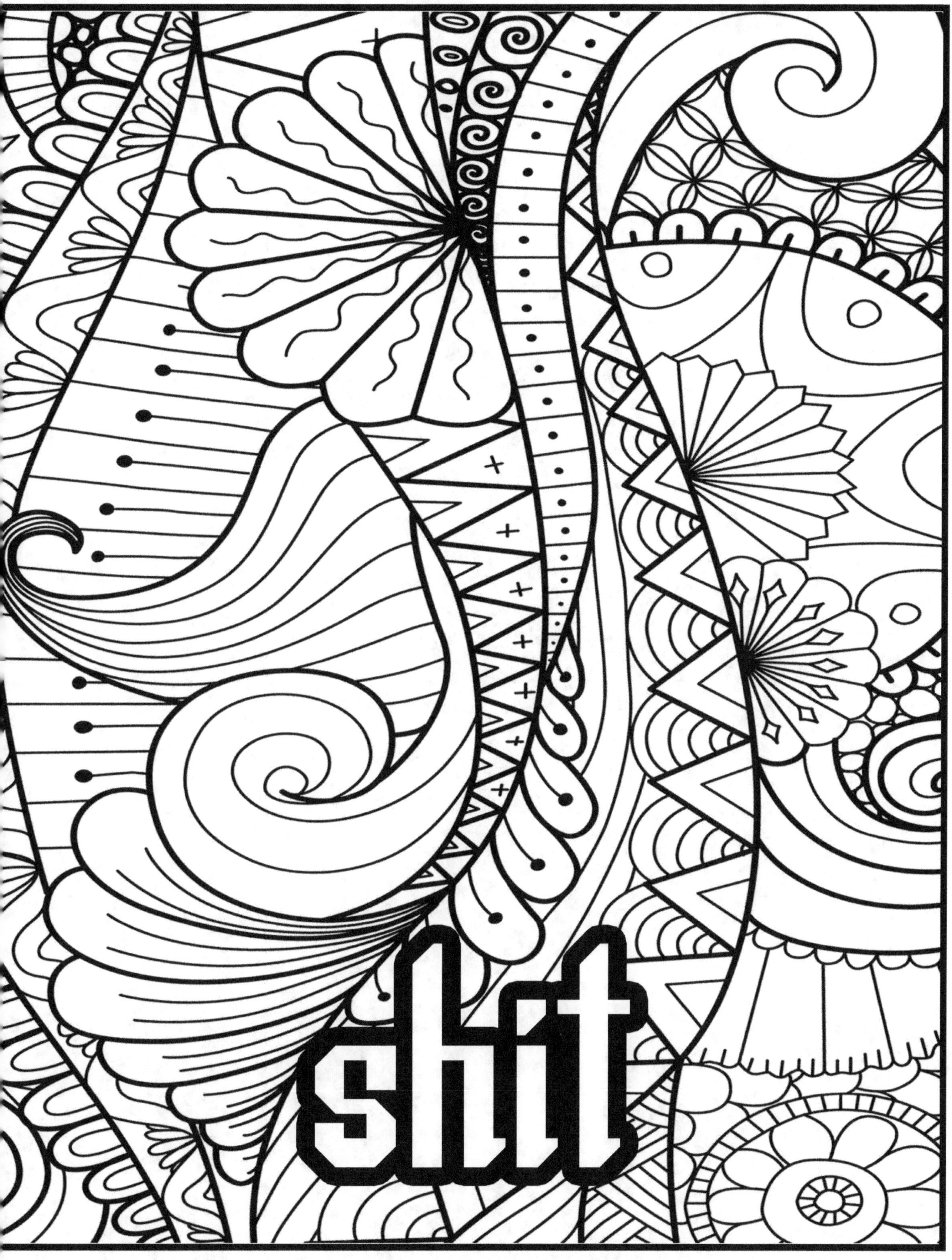
shit

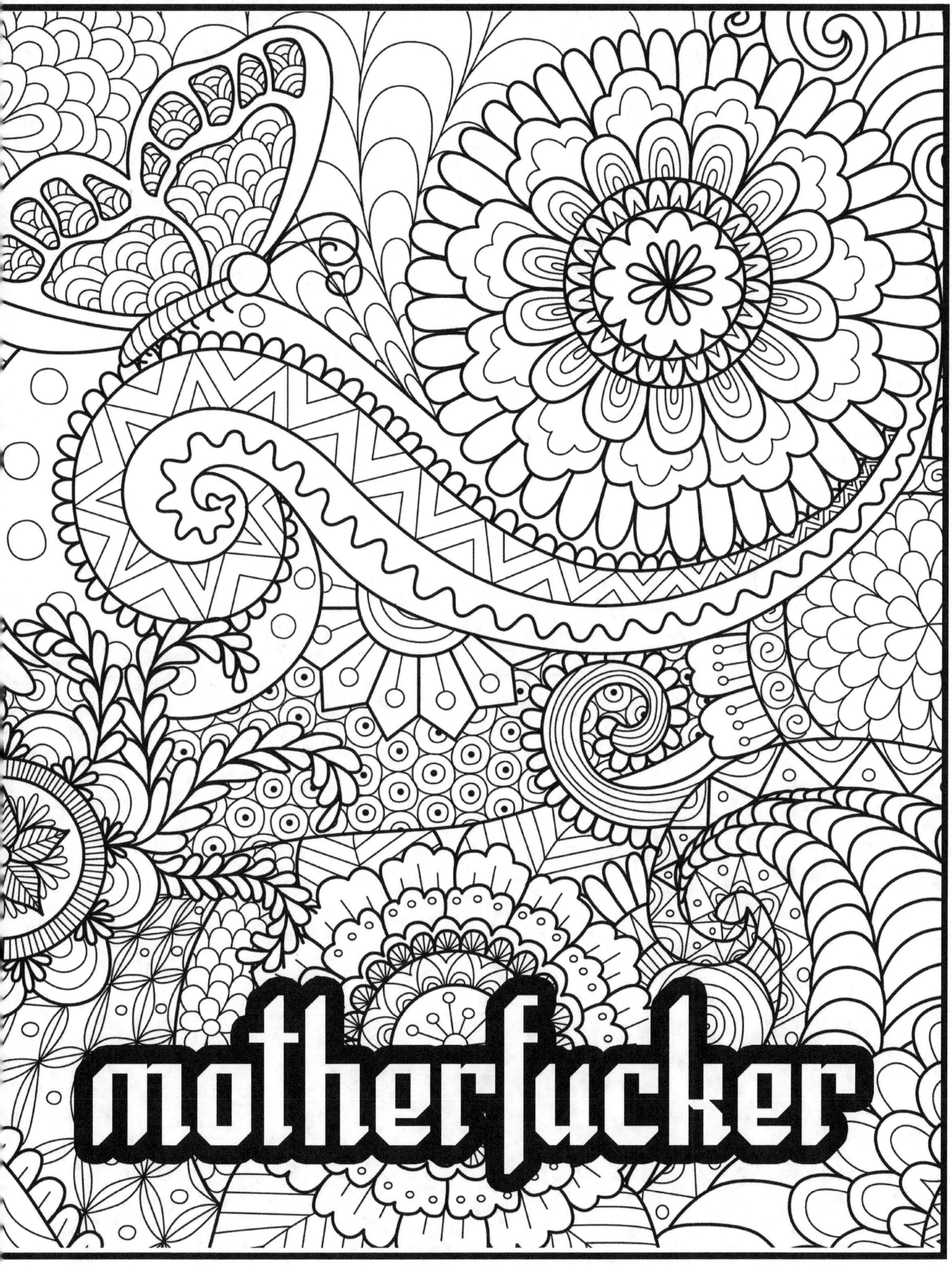
motherfucker

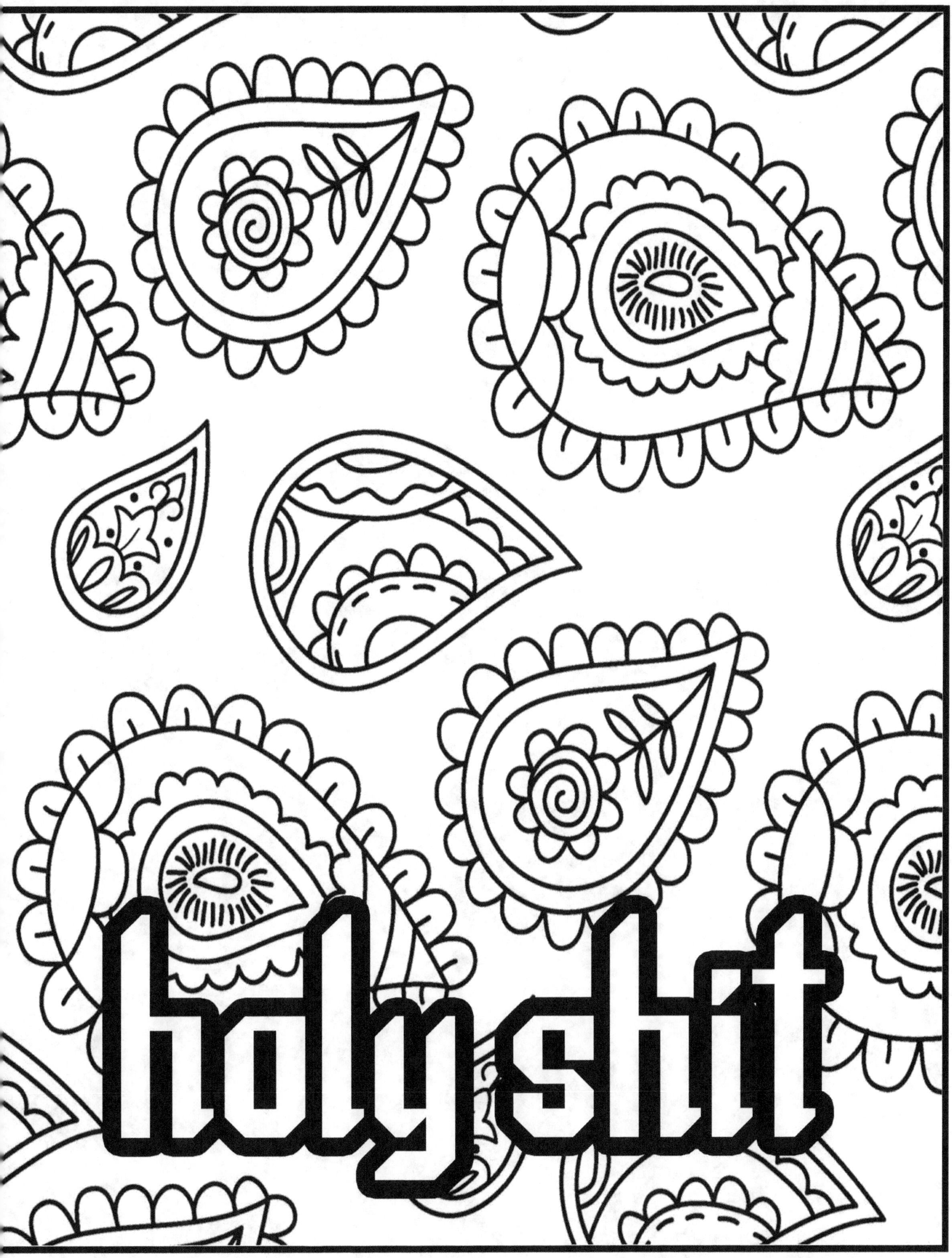
holy shit

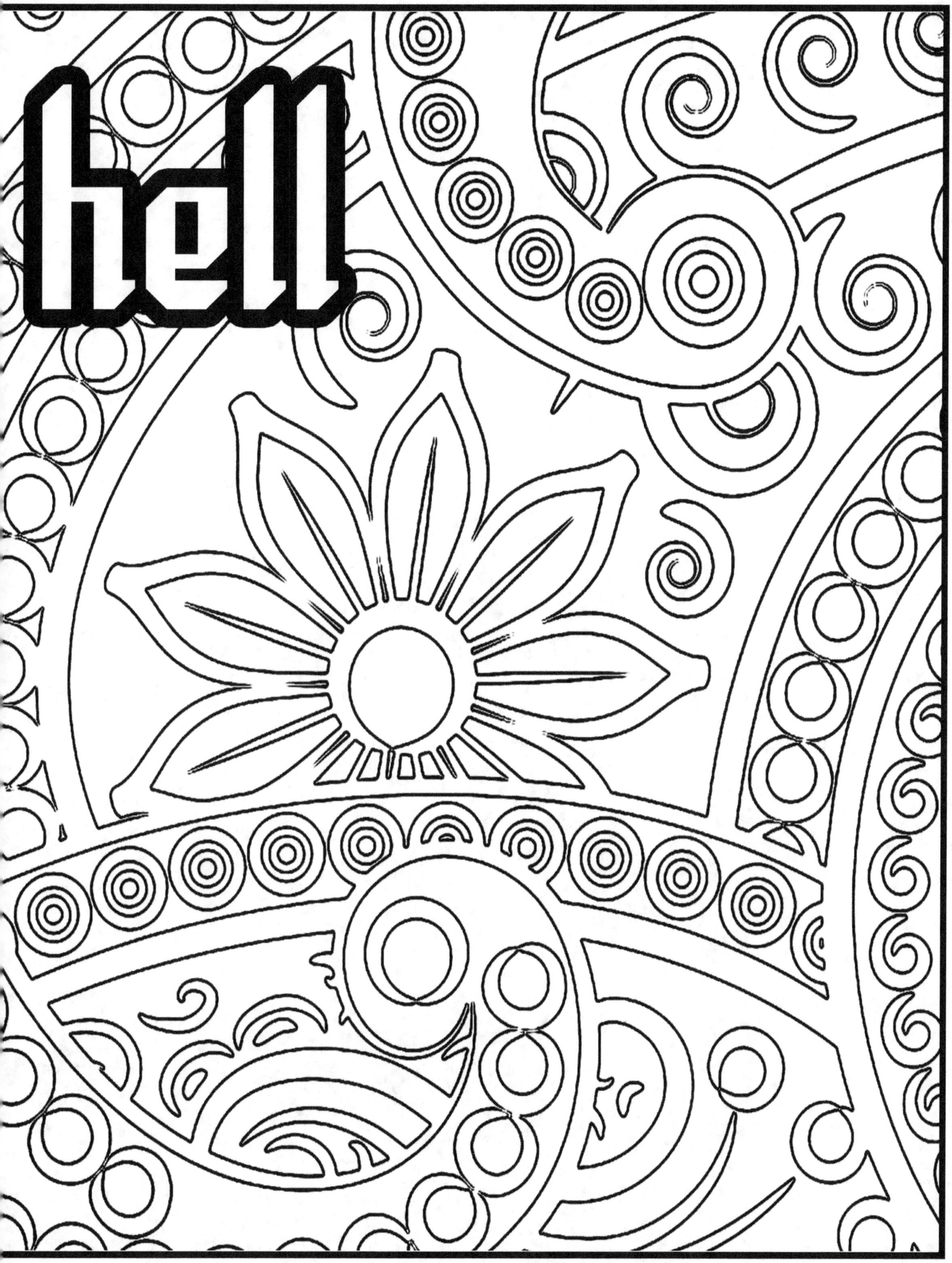
hell

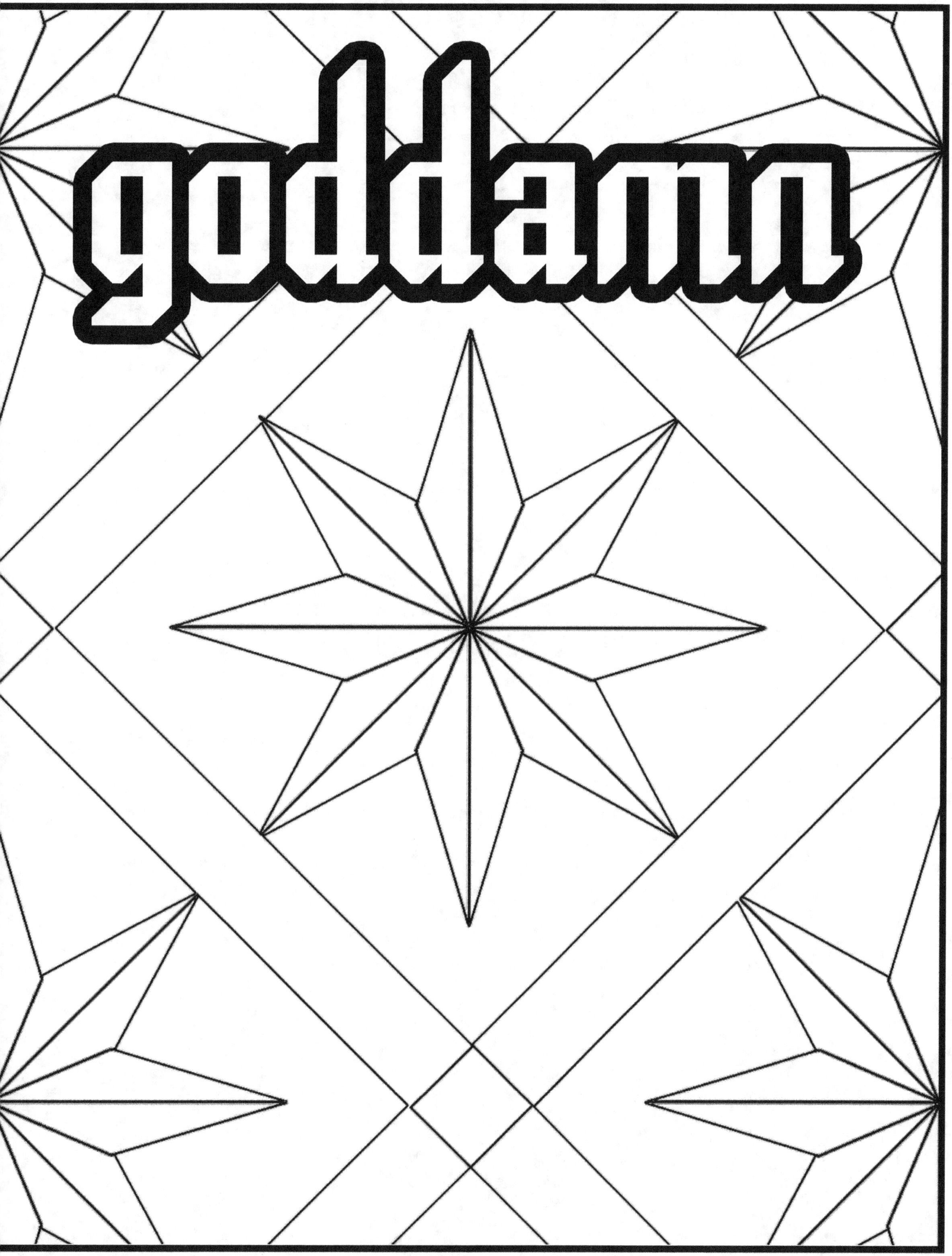
goddamn

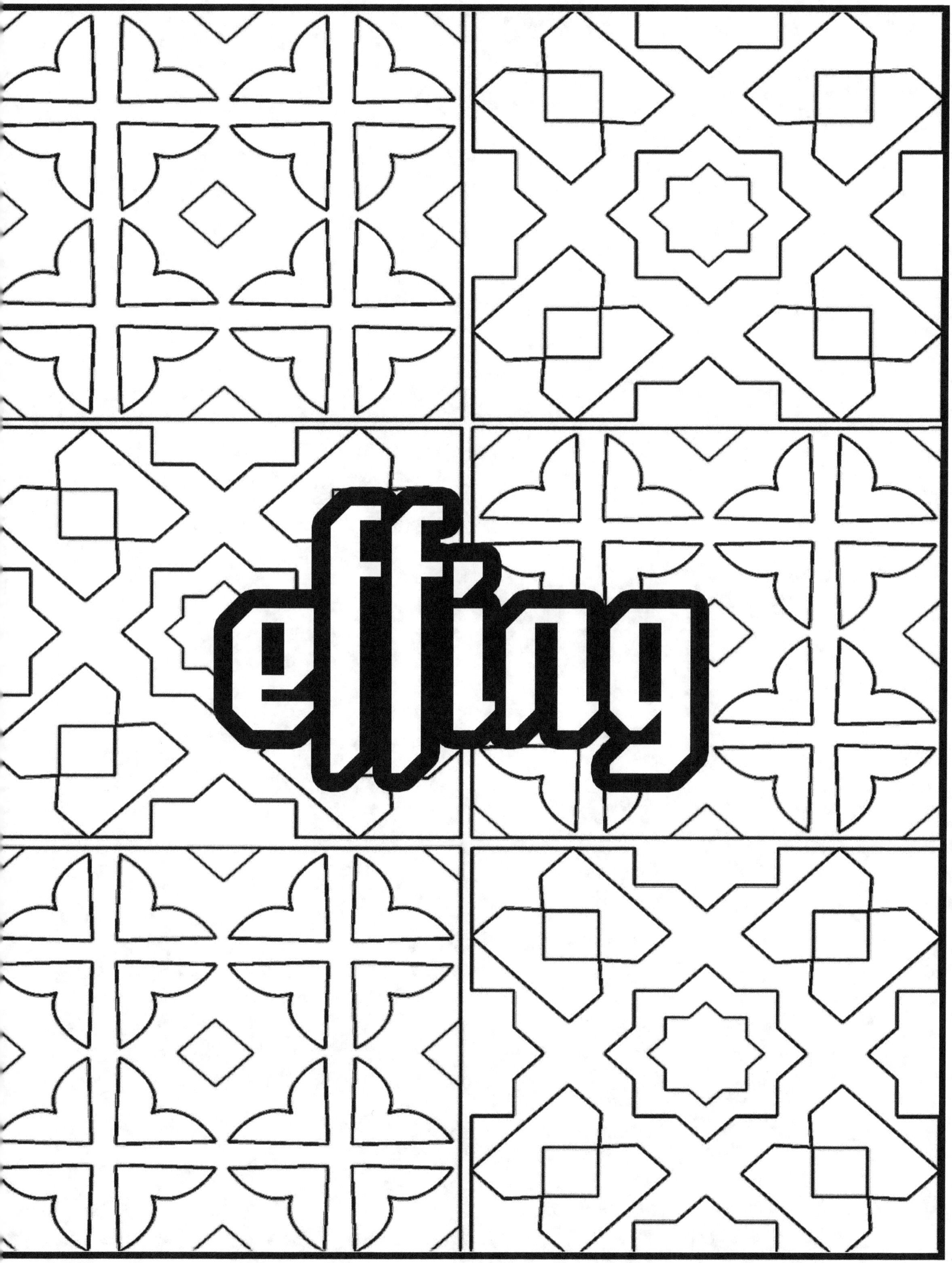
effing

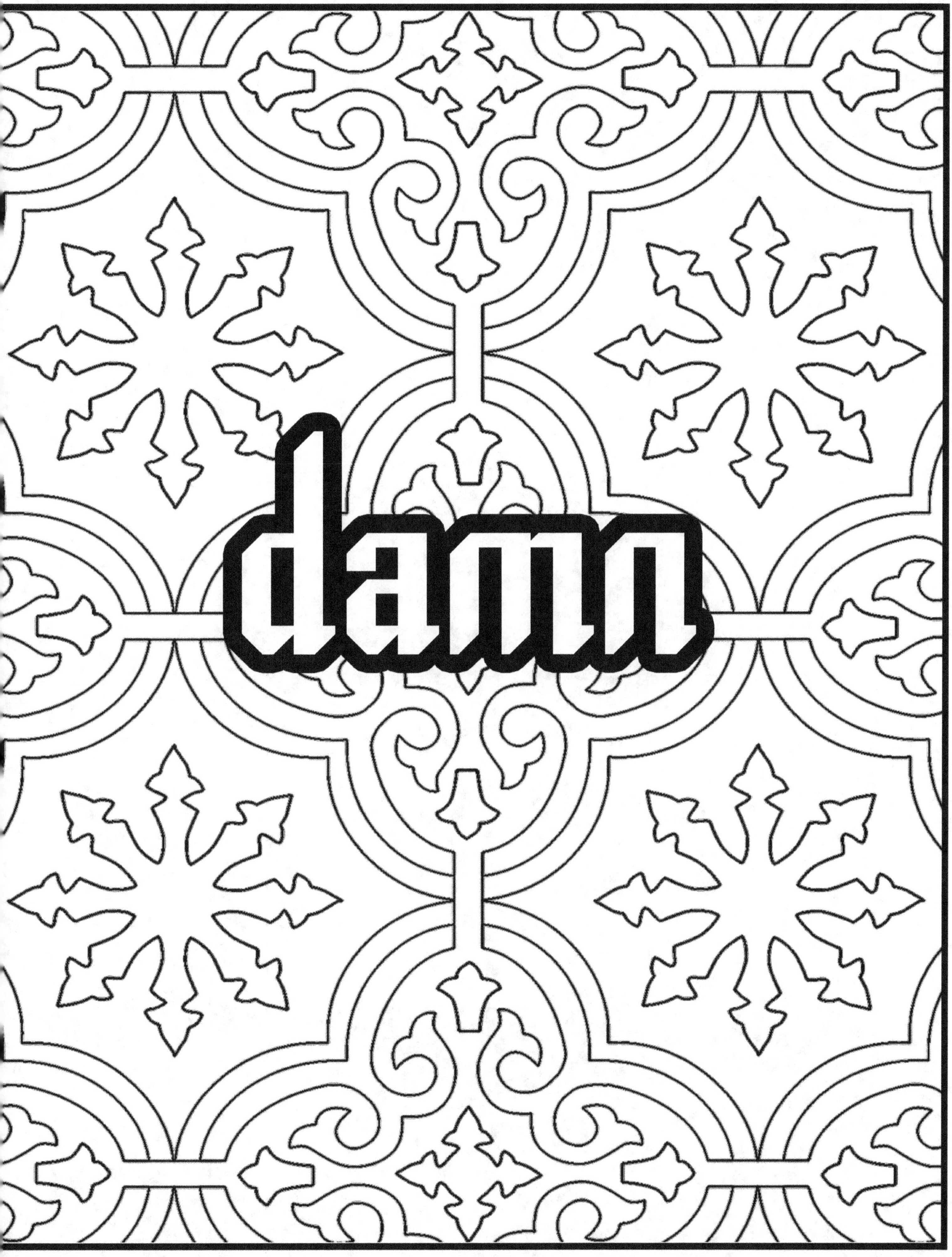
damn

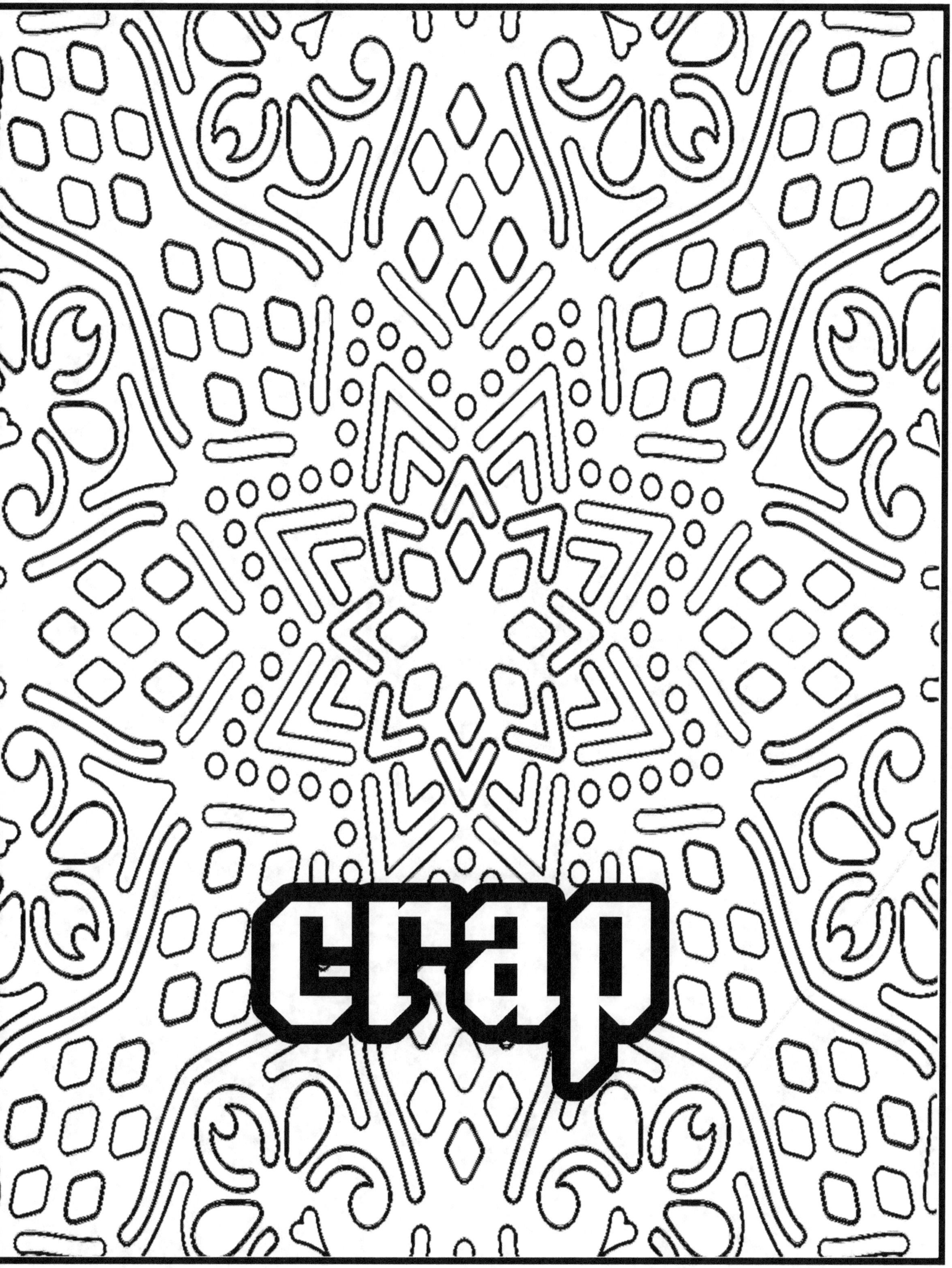
crap

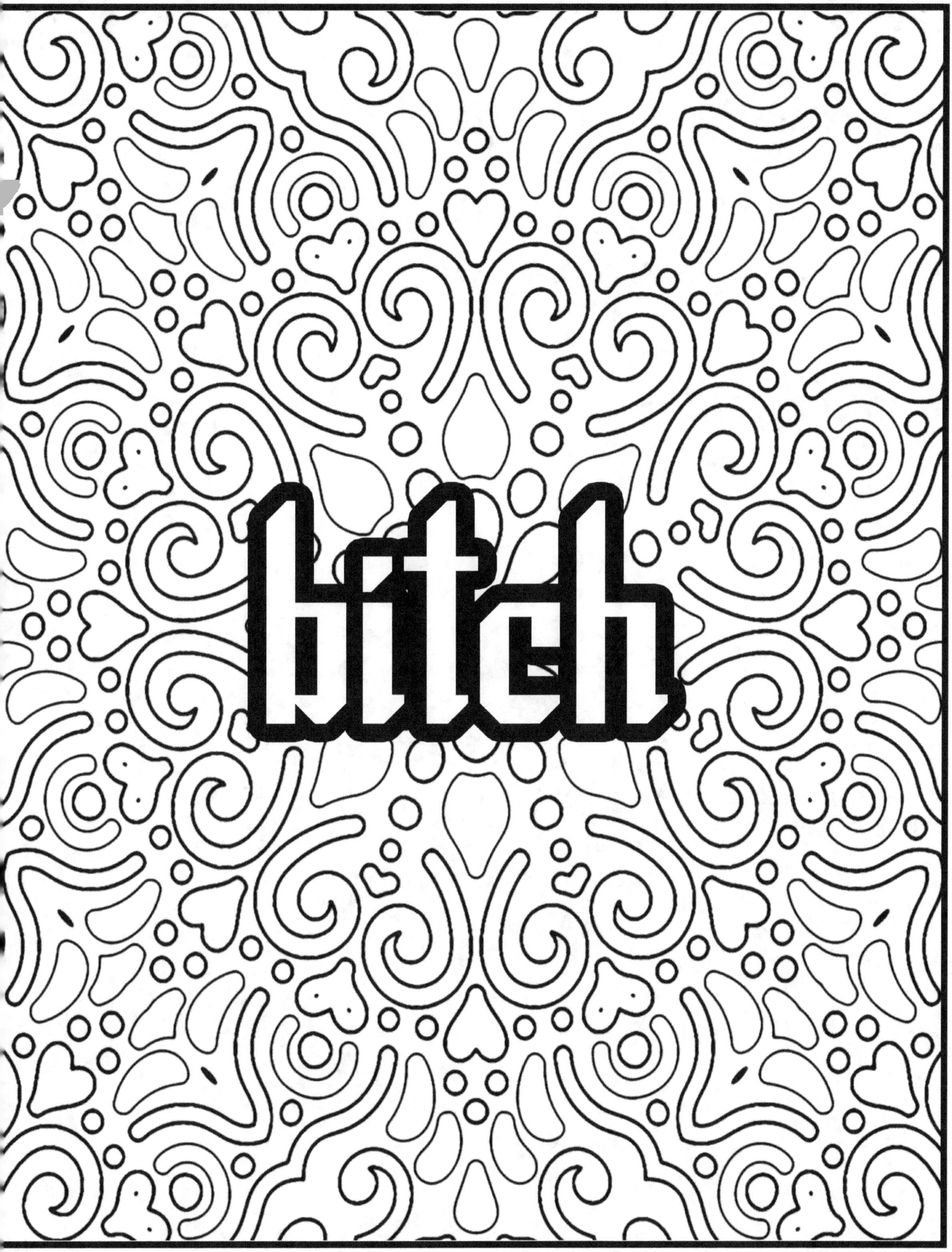
bitch

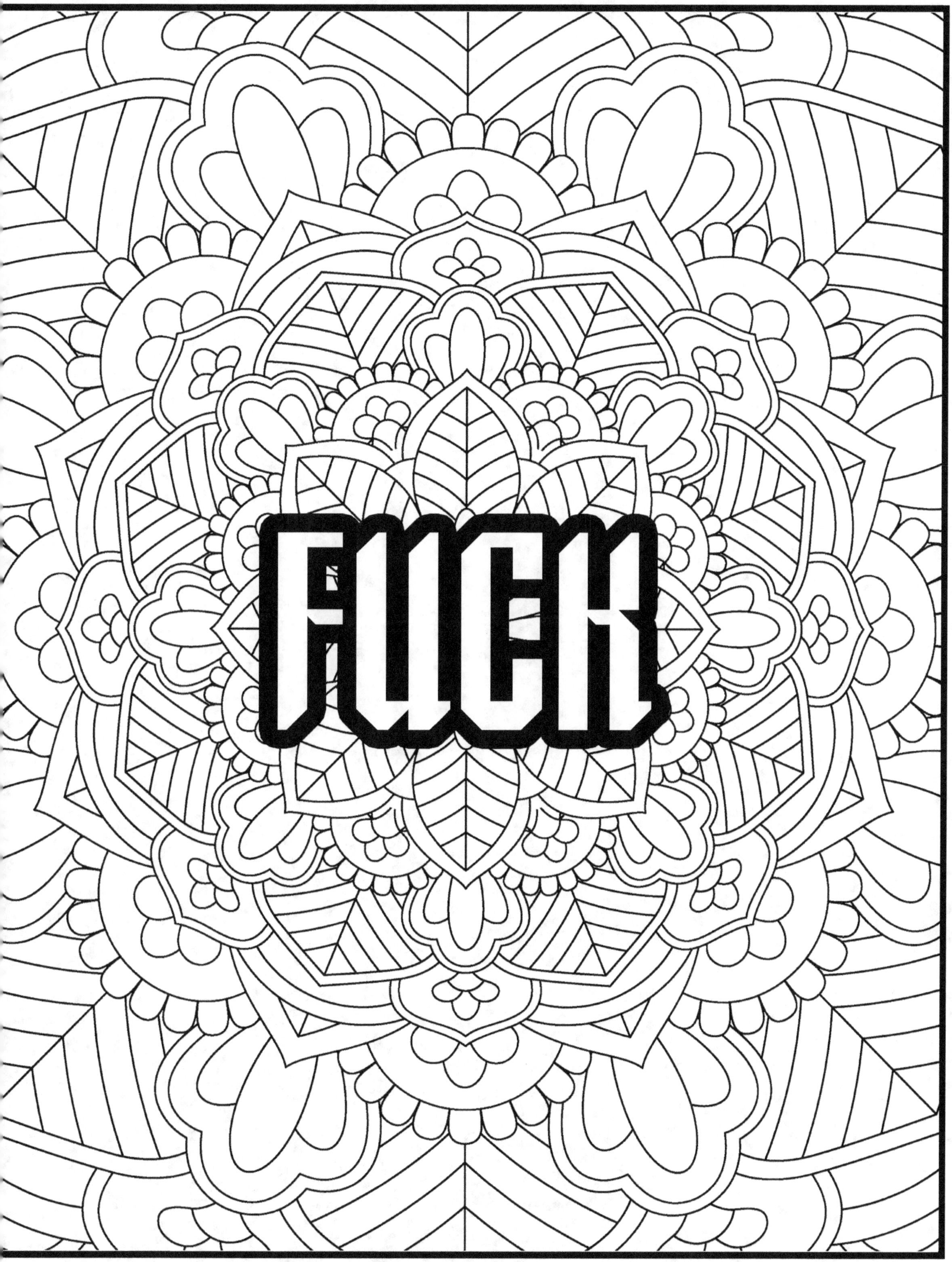
FUCK

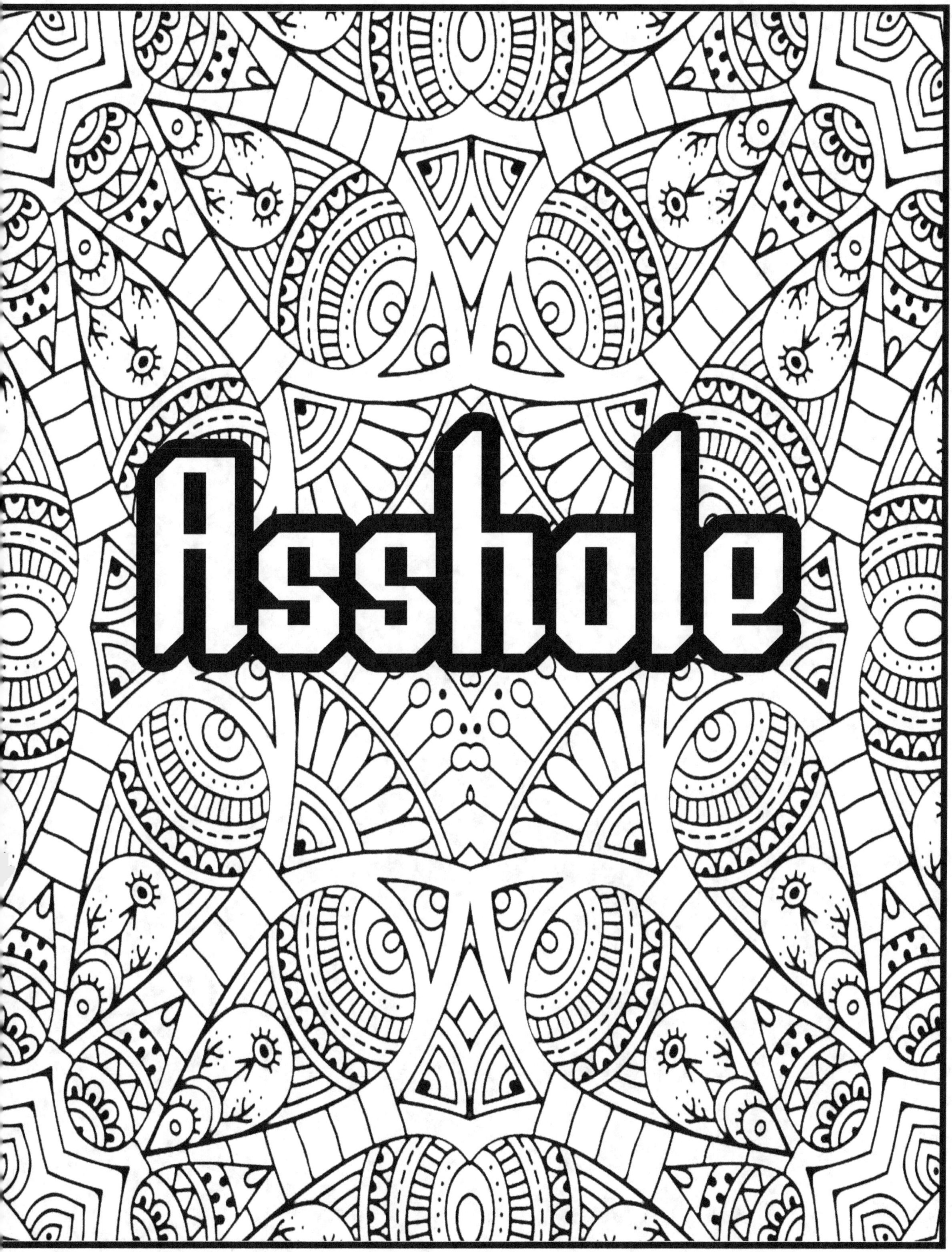
Asshole

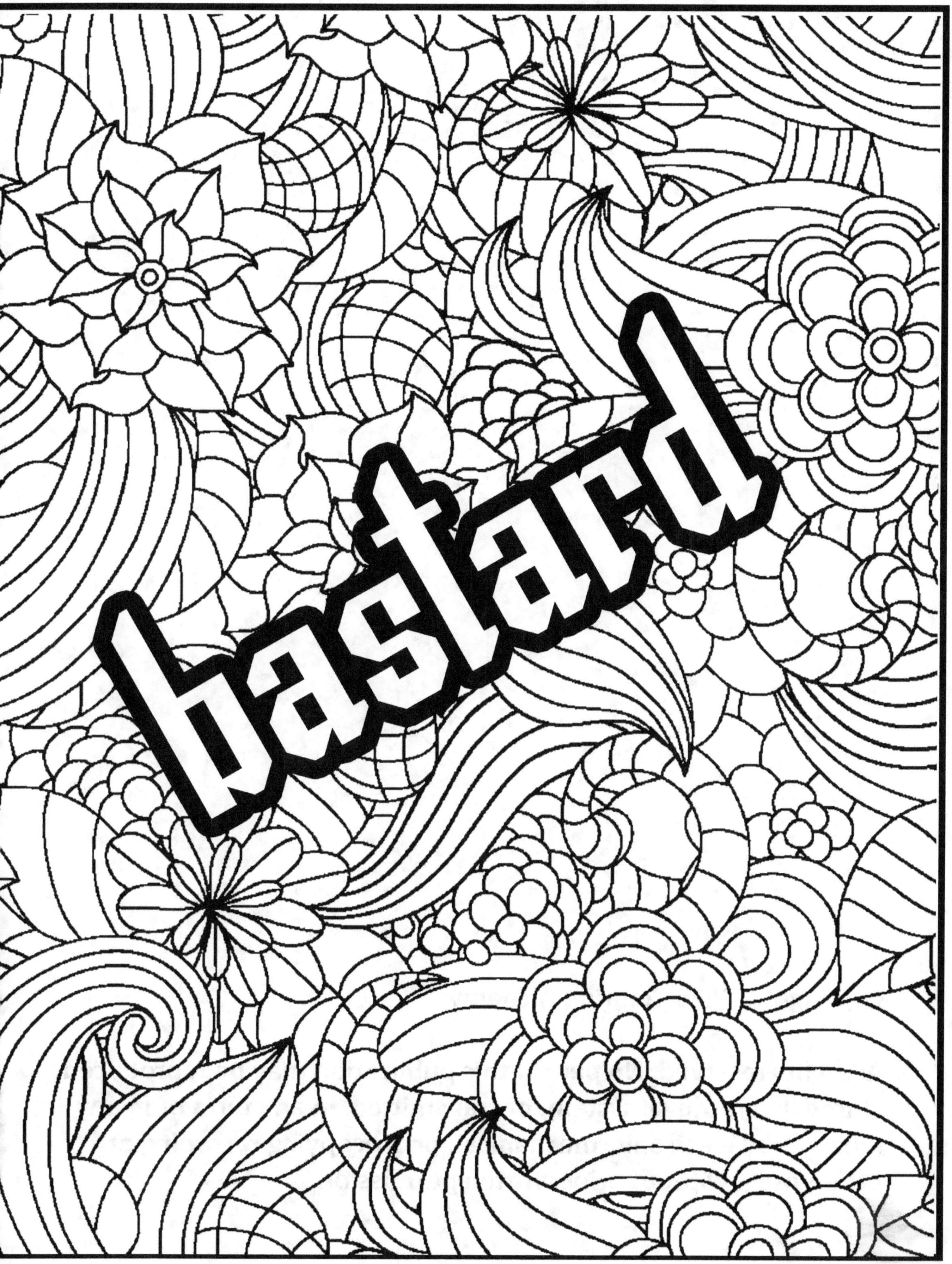
bastard

www.ingramcontent.com/pod-product-compliance
Lightning Source LLC
Chambersburg PA
CBHW081538220526
45467CB00010B/3244